Diego Rivera

A Proud Heritage The Hispanic Library

Diego Rivera

Painting Mexico

Deborah Kent

Content Adviser: Cesáreo Moreno
Visual Arts Director
Mexican Fine Arts Center Museum
Chicago, Illinois

Published in the United States of America by The Child's World®
PO Box 326 • Chanhassen, MN 55317-0326 • 800-599-READ • www.childsworld.com

Acknowledgments
The Child's World®: Mary Berendes, Publishing Director

Editorial Directions, Inc.: E. Russell Primm, Editorial Director; Pam Rosenberg, Project Editor;
Katie Marsico, Associate Editor; Matt Messbarger, Editorial Assistant; Susan Hindman,
Copyeditor; Lucia Raatma, Proofreader; Molly Symmonds, Fact Checker; Timothy Griffin/
IndexServ, Indexer; Dawn Friedman, Photo Researcher; Linda S. Koutris, Photo Selector

Creative Spark: Mary Francis and Rob Court, Design and Page Production

Cartography by XNR Productions, Inc.

Photos
Cover: detail from Self-Portrait, January 1941, by Diego Rivera, oil on canvas, 24 x 16 7/8
in. (61 x 43 cm). Courtesy of Smith College Museum of Art, Northampton, Massachusetts,
Gift of Irene Rich Clifford, 1977, and copyright 2004 Banco de México, Diego Rivera &
Frida Kahlo Museums Trust, Av. Cinco de Mayo No. 2, Col. Centro, Del. Cuauhtémoc 06059,
México, D.F.

Erich Lessing/Art Resource, NY: 16; Schalkwijk/Art Resource, NY and copyright 2004
Banco de México, Diego Rivera & Frida Kahlo Museums Trust: 23, 27, 32; Kelly-Mooney
Photography/Corbis: 7; Dave G. Houser/Corbis: 8; Bettmann/Corbis: 9, 25, 26, 29, 34, 36;
Danny Lehman/Corbis: 11; Danny Lehman/Corbis and copyright 2004 Banco de México,
Diego Rivera & Frida Kahlo Museums Trust: 24; Roger Tidman/Corbis: 13; Corbis: 17, 20;
Araldo de Luca/Corbis: 21; Hulton-Deutsch Collection/Corbis: 31; Detroit Industry, South
Wall, 1932-33 by Diego M. Rivera, Gift of Edsel B. Ford, photograph copyright 2001 the
Detroit Institute of Arts: 28; Hulton|Archive/Getty Images: 10, 15, 33.

Library of Congress Cataloging-in-Publication Data
Kent, Deborah.
  Diego Rivera : painting Mexico / by Deborah Kent
      p. cm. — (A proud heritage)
  Includes index.
    ISBN 1-59296-384-6 (library bound : alk. paper)
  1. Rivera, Diego, 1886-1957—Juvenile literature. 2. Painters—Mexico—Biography—
Juvenile literature. I. Title. II. Proud heritage (Child's World (Firm))
  ND259.R5K44 2005
  759.972—dc22
                                    2004018046

Chapter One

The Boy Who Painted Walls

The Anahuacalli Museum is one of the most remarkable buildings in Mexico City. Its walls, made from rough volcanic stone, form a huge pyramid. Arched entrances lead into a maze of galleries. Displayed throughout the building are thousands of ancient statues. These figures represent the gods and goddesses of the Aztecs, Mayas, and other people of ancient Mexico.

Diego Rivera, Mexico's most famous artist, designed this amazing building. He filled it with objects of ancient art that he collected over his lifetime. Rivera donated the building and its contents to the Mexican people. He will always be remembered for this extraordinary gift. Yet he is known best of all for his **murals.** Diego Rivera was one of the greatest muralists of the 20th century.

Many beautiful works of art are on display at the Anahuacalli Museum.

Diego Rivera was born on December 8, 1886, in the city of Guanajuato, Mexico. Diego had a twin brother, Carlos, who died when he was less than 2 years old. Diego's mother grew depressed after Carlos's death. She sent Diego to live with his nurse, Antonia, a Tarascan Indian. She took Diego to her remote mountain village. Years later, Diego claimed that while he lived with Antonia, he learned the ways of the forest and its

Diego Rivera was born in this house in Guanajuato, Mexico. The building is now used as a museum.

creatures. He said that even the snakes and jaguars became his friends.

By the time he was three, Diego was back in Guanajuato. He loved to play in his father's study, where he found a ready supply of paper and pencils. He would climb onto his father's desk and draw pictures on any sheet of paper he saw. Now and then, he even drew on the walls. Finally, Diego's father set up a special room for his son's artwork. Black canvas cloth covered the walls, and Diego had plenty of chalk. The taller he grew, the higher his drawings reached. He drew trains, animals, and people. He drew the moon and the stars, the balconied houses along his street, and the mountains that loomed over the city.

Business was not going well for Diego's father, Diego Rivera Sr. He decided to make a new start in life. In 1892, the family moved to Mexico City, the nation's capital. Diego's father worked in the government of President Porfirio Díaz.

Soon after he arrived in Mexico City, little Diego fell gravely ill. During his long recovery, he read dozens of books in his father's library. Books about

Pan o Palo

Diego Rivera grew up during the rule of Porfirio Díaz. Díaz became president of Mexico in 1877. He encouraged mining and the production of sugar and tobacco. He also built thousands of miles of railroads.

At the same time, however, Díaz was a cruel dictator. His motto was *pan o palo,* meaning "bread or the club." Those who obeyed him were rewarded, and those who disobeyed were killed. During Díaz's 30 years in power, millions of Mexicans lived in virtual slavery.

A Mexico City street scene from the 1890s includes a view of the National Theatre of Mexico. Diego Rivera's family moved to Mexico City in 1892.

warfare were his favorites. He spent hours drawing soldiers and cannons and making maps of historic battlefields.

Diego's father was thrilled by his son's interest in military matters. When Diego was 10, he was sent to a military school. It was soon clear that, although he liked to draw soldiers, Diego was not cut out to become one. He hated the drills and the strict rules at school. After a week, he fled to his home. "I won't go back!" he told his parents. "I hate it! I beg you not to send me back."

After his failure at military school, Diego knew for certain what he wanted to be. He asked his parents to let him take art classes. Neither of his parents thought that art was a wise career choice, but at last they gave in to Diego's pleading. When he was 11, Diego enrolled at the San Carlos Academy of Fine Arts in Mexico City.

Sculptures on display at the San Carlos Academy of Fine Arts in Mexico City.

Normally, students younger than 16 were not admitted. Diego was the youngest student at the school. He was big for his age, which helped him fit in with the older boys. Nevertheless, they often teased him mercilessly. "Let them," counseled Diego's favorite teacher. "I do not know whether you will ever amount to anything. But you look carefully, and you have something in your head."

Diego left San Carlos when he was 16 and set out to earn his living as a painter. He traveled the countryside, painting landscapes and portraits. A number of his paintings sold, but Diego was not satisfied with his work. He knew he had much more to learn. Diego longed to study in Europe, where he could see the works of some of the world's master painters.

In 1906, Diego's father went to the Mexican state of Veracruz to visit the governor on business. The governor, Teodoro Dehesa, supported education and the arts in Veracruz. Diego's father showed the governor several of his son's paintings, and Dehesa was impressed. He offered to support Diego while he studied art in Europe. He asked only that Diego send examples of his work to show his progress.

A few months before Diego left for Europe, **textile** workers in Veracruz went out on strike. For years, the workers had earned so little that they were constantly in debt to their employers. Now, when they refused to go to work, the factory owners turned to the national government for help.

Porfirio Díaz sent troops to put down the rebellion. Soldiers rode into the crowd of strikers, shooting down women, children, and men. Diego Rivera never forgot the horror of this attack. In years to come, it proved to be a major influence in his life and in his art.

Diego Rivera hoped to study art in Europe where he could see great works of art at famous museums such as the Prado Museum (below) in Madrid, Spain.

Chapter Two

In the Footsteps of the Masters

"I study and paint from the time I get up until I go to bed," Diego Rivera wrote to his father from Spain. "This ought to continue still for some eight months before I can stop working so hard."

Rivera soon realized, however, that eight months of hard work would barely begin his artistic education. The more he painted, the more unhappy he became. He studied the works of Spanish masters such as El Greco, Goya, and Velázquez and tried to imitate their styles. His friends and teachers praised him, but still he felt he was not good enough.

After a year in Spain, Rivera traveled to Belgium, The Netherlands, England, and France. In London, he met a young Russian artist, Angelina Beloff. Angelina quickly became a close friend, and she and Rivera married two years later. Rivera later described

Diego Rivera enjoyed spending time at sidewalk cafés in Paris, France.

Angelina as "a kind, sensitive, almost unbelievably decent person [who] much to her misfortune became my wife."

When Rivera traveled to Paris in 1909, he was dazzled by the city with its broad streets, sunlit gardens, and sidewalk cafés. Most exciting of all were the city's countless art galleries. One day, he caught sight of a painting that brought him to a stop. The artist was

Paul Cézanne, a French painter known for his magical use of light and color. All day, Rivera walked up and down in front of the gallery, gazing at Cézanne's work. Cézanne inspired him to explore new possibilities in his own painting.

In 1910, Rivera returned to Mexico for several months. The country was celebrating the 100th anniversary of the beginning of the War of Independence and its freedom from Spain. Rivera had been invited to display some of his paintings at a **centennial** exhibit. While he was in Mexico, President Porfirio Díaz was overthrown by rebels. Mexico plunged into a bloody war, the Mexican Revolution, which lasted for the next 10 years.

When Rivera returned to Europe in the spring of 1911, he settled in Paris. He worked long hours in his studio, but as daylight faded he headed to the cafés.

Paul Cezanne painted the still life Apples and Oranges *in the late 1890s.*

The Mexican Revolution of 1910–1920 was the first revolution fought in the 20th century and the bloodiest war ever fought in the Americas. More than 1 million soldiers and civilians

lost their lives. One leader after another took control, only to be overthrown. One man held office for only 45 minutes!

Paris lured artists, writers, and musicians from all over the world. They gathered in cafés to talk about politics, philosophy, and art.

Rivera's huge, bearded figure was soon familiar to everyone. Rivera was more than 6 feet (2 meters) tall and weighed about 300 pounds (136 kilograms). He was large in other ways as well. He compelled attention with his intense emotions and his irresistible flow of stories. From a few pebbles of truth, Rivera could build a castle of tall tales. He told his listeners that he had plotted to assassinate Porfirio Díaz and had attacked military trains for the Revolution. He even claimed that he had once dined on human flesh. To the Europeans, Rivera was wild and exotic, a traveler from an unknown land.

Rivera experimented with many painting styles. Sometimes he created lifelike portraits or landscapes with mountains and clouds. For a few years, he painted in a popular new style called cubism. Cubist painters broke images into geometric shapes. They saw their work as a response to a world in which machines had power over nature.

These carefree years ended abruptly in 1914, when Europe plunged into World War I (1914–1918). War still raged in Mexico as well, and Rivera's checks from Veracruz came to a stop. Rivera sold enough paintings to pay the rent and put simple meals on the table most of the time. There were days, however, when he and Angelina went hungry.

No matter what happened in the wider world, Rivera went on with his work. At times, he painted in a **frenzy,** not stopping to eat or sleep. In 1917, when Angelina told him that a baby was on the way, Rivera was horrified. "If the child disturbs me, I'll throw it out the window!" he cried. Nothing and no one would stand in the way of his art. Rivera's son, Diego Maria

Angel Rivera, died of pneumonia while he was still a toddler. After little Diego's death, Rivera and Angelina gradually drifted apart.

In 1917, a Communist revolution in Russia destroyed the power of the czars, the emperors who had ruled the country for centuries. The Communists promised to give power to the people of Russia. Rivera knew many Russians in Paris. Most of them were

Diego Rivera was born in Mexico, but as a young man, he traveled to many countries in Europe. He settled in Paris, France, and lived there for about 10 years.

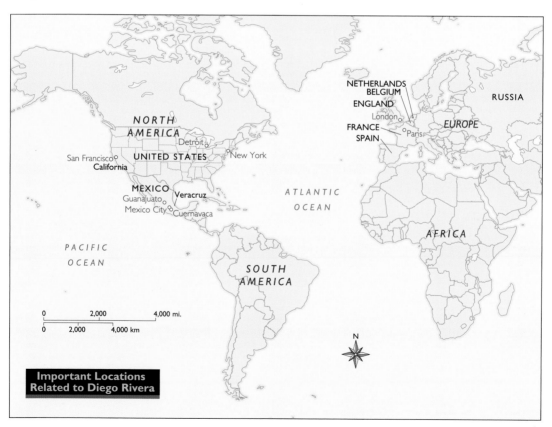

Important Locations Related to Diego Rivera

filled with hope about communism, and Rivera shared their excitement.

World War I ended on November 11, 1918. In the years after the war, Rivera became increasingly interested in the art of the **Renaissance.** During the Renaissance, architects designed majestic churches and cathedrals. Renaissance artists adorned them with sculptures and

To Each According to His Need

The Communists claimed that they would provide for each person according to his need and take from each according to his ability. They would distribute money and resources equally among all of the people. In reality, however, communism imposed rigid rules that stifled individual freedom. After the Communist Revolution of 1917, Russia was reborn as the Union of Soviet Socialist Republics (USSR). Many educated people in Europe and the U.S. were enthusiastic about the Russian Revolution. But over time, most of them became disillusioned with communism.

In the 1920s, Diego Rivera became interested in works of art from the Renaissance, such as this fresco Hannibal Fighting a Roman Legion in the Alps.

paintings, creating monumental art for monumental buildings. Many of the works Rivera admired were **frescoes.** Rivera loved the idea that this artwork was made to be viewed by everyone, rich and poor alike.

In 1921, Rivera returned to Mexico and assured Angelina that he would send for her when he was settled. Angelina never rejoined him. Their marriage had come to an end.

Art with a Message

Rivera's ship docked in Veracruz, and from there he took a train through the mountains to Mexico City. Enchanted, he gazed from the windows at the passing forests, fields, and villages. At each stop, he drank in the colors of flowers and fruits. He noted the strength and patience in the faces of the people. Later he wrote, "I was struck by the inexpressible beauty of that rich and severe, wretched and **exuberant** land."

After 10 years of bloodshed, the Mexican Revolution was finally at an end. Despite the long war, Mexico was still a land where a few wealthy families ruled over millions of poor people. Yet the revolution had brought about some changes. Jose Vasconcelos, the new commissioner of education, was working to promote **literacy** in Mexico. He encouraged the construction of schools all over the country.

Creation *was painted by Diego Rivera in the auditorium of the National Preparatory School in Mexico City.*

Vasconcelos wanted murals to decorate the walls of many of these schools. Among the painters he chose were three who became Mexico's great muralists: David Siqueiros, José Clemente Orozco, and Diego Rivera.

Rivera's first assignment was a mural in the auditorium of the National Preparatory School in Mexico City. He was never satisfied with the picture, which represented the Creation. Vasconcelos thought it was splendid. He asked Rivera to paint a series of murals

Detail from Fraternity, *a mural painted by Diego Rivera between 1923 and 1928.*

for the Ministry of Education building. Rivera decided to paint frescoes, though he had never used the technique before. Sometimes he was overwhelmed with frustration. One evening, one of his assistants found him "sobbing uncontrollably and furiously erasing his entire day's work with a little trowel, like a small boy in a rage flattening his sand castle." After many experiments, Rivera mastered the art of fresco, and it became one of his favorite methods of painting.

In 1922, Rivera married Lupe Marín, a woman who served as a model for several of his paintings. They had two daughters, Lupe and Ruth. Lupe Marín shared Rivera's political views. When Rivera joined the Communist Party in 1923, she was at his side. Rivera used his murals to convey his Communist ideas. Many show the humble Mexican people being **exploited** by the rich and later being **liberated** in a future classless society.

Rivera was deeply disappointed, however, when he visited Communist Russia in 1927. A powerful dictator, Joseph Stalin, had just taken over the country. Stalin's secret police arrested anyone who spoke out against the government. In Stalin's Russia, no artist had the right to free expression. Back in Mexico, Rivera fell into disagreements with members of the Communist Party. Despite these disagreements, Rivera continued to explore themes of class struggle in his work.

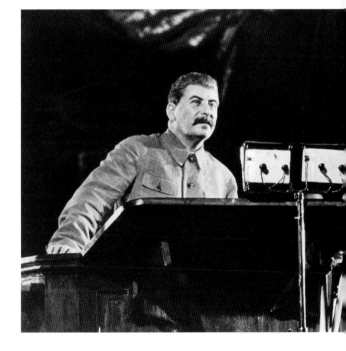

Joseph Stalin was born in 1879. He died in 1953 at the age of 73.

Rivera and Lupe Marín were divorced in 1927. That same year, a young painter named Frida Kahlo asked Rivera to look at some of her work. Rivera liked the paintings and was intrigued by the painter. The two artists were married on August 21, 1929. Their marriage was a stormy one. They divorced, only to remarry a year later. Rivera had relationships with

A Life in Portraits

Frida Kahlo grew up in Coyoacán, a suburb of Mexico City. At 18, she was severely injured in a bus accident, and during her recovery she began to paint. Most of Kahlo's paintings are self-portraits reflecting her inner and outer life. A few months before she died, she had a solo exhibition in Mexico City. She arrived by ambulance and greeted her admirers from her bed.

many women through-
out his life, but Frida
Kahlo was by far the
most important to him.

By now, Rivera was
busily at work on two
vast murals, one at the
National Palace in Mexico
City and the other in
the Palace of Cortés
in Cuernavaca. As his
fame spread, he re-
ceived invitations to
paint in the United
States. In 1931, he
painted a mural for the

Detail from The Conquest, *painted by Diego Rivera at the National Palace in Mexico City.*

Pacific Stock Exchange in San Francisco, California.
The American public was enchanted by the enormous
Mexican man in boots and cowboy hat who clung to a
scaffold and brought the walls of the stock exchange
to life.

After a wildly successful exhibit at New York's
Museum of Modern Art, Rivera moved on to a major
project in Detroit. He had been hired to paint murals
for the Detroit Institute of Arts. Detroit was the capital

Detroit Industry *is considered by many to be one of Rivera's best works. The south wall of the mural is pictured above.*

of America's automobile industry. As a Communist, Rivera had raised an outcry against the exploitation of industrial workers. Now he saw large-scale factories for the first time, and he was filled with admiration.

He decided that the auto industry was "as beautiful as the early Aztec or Mayan sculpture." Rivera decided to paint scenes from a Ford Motor plant. The panels show welders, painters, and assembly-line workers in vivid detail. The mural at the Detroit Institute is considered one of Rivera's most outstanding works.

Rivera's Communist friends were outraged by his celebration of private industry. When Rivera agreed to paint a mural for the RCA Building at New York's Rockefeller Center, they were even more dismayed. The Rockefellers were among the richest families in the world. They had built their empire from the labor of thousands of poorly paid workers. But Rivera had not forgotten his Communist zeal. The new mural, *Man at the Crossroads,* included a prominent portrait of the Communist leader Vladimir Lenin.

The Rockefellers told Rivera to paint out Lenin's portrait. When Rivera refused, they ordered him to stop his work completely. A few months later, workers chipped the mural from the wall.

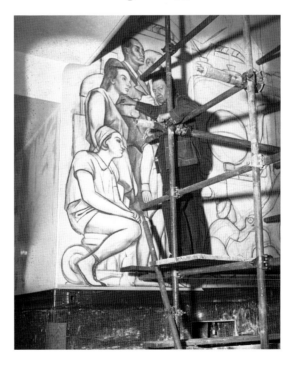

Diego Rivera at work on his mural for the RCA Building in 1933.

Diego Rivera was devastated. He felt betrayed by the country that had made him feel so welcome. Deeply discouraged, he headed home to Mexico City.

Chapter Four

The Aztec Palace

In Mexico City, Rivera tried to re-create the Rockefeller Center mural on the wall of a government building. The result was flat and lifeless. The artist sank into despair. To bring in money, he painted portraits and Mexican scenes. His pictures provided him with a comfortable income, yet he yearned for more important work.

He found it in the political arena. In 1937, he joined a group of Communists who opposed the regime of Joseph Stalin. Rivera became concerned with the plight of the Russian Communist leader Leon Trotsky. Trotsky had broken with Stalin and fled Russia to escape Stalin's secret police. Rivera helped to arrange for Trotsky to obtain political asylum, or refuge, in Mexico.

Trotsky and his wife reached Mexico City in 1938, and they lived as guests in the home of Rivera and

Leon Trotsky was born in 1879 in Yanovka, Ukraine.

Frida Kahlo. For several months, all went smoothly. Eventually, however, Trotsky and Rivera quarreled, and the Russian couple moved out. Soon after, the secret police caught up with Trotsky. He was assassinated near Mexico City on August 20, 1940.

Discouraged about the present, Rivera turned more and more to the past for his inspiration. At the National

The Tarascan Civilization *was Rivera's idealized view of the life of Mexico's people before the arrival of the Spanish conquistadores.*

Palace, he painted scenes of Mexican life before the coming of the Spaniards. His paintings show happy Native Americans tilling fields, harvesting crops, and dancing in splendid costumes. These panels celebrate an idealized Mexican past, before the influence of Europeans. Later scenes portray the brutality of the Spanish conquerors. The once-happy Indians are beaten, murdered, and enslaved.

In 1942, Rivera began to construct a palace of his own. The design used elements from ancient Aztec temples and palaces, enhanced by Rivera's endlessly rich imagination. In the maze of galleries, corridors, and courtyards, Rivera displayed his vast collection of **pre-Columbian** artwork.

When he wasn't at his Aztec palace, Rivera spent most of his time at the Blue House with Frida Kahlo. This house in Coyoacán was Frida's birthplace. Its patios were filled with flowers, birds, and sunlight. Frida adored animals and kept a variety of pets. "Nobody had a stranger household than the Riveras," wrote a visitor. "There were monkeys jumping through the window at lunchtime. They just jumped up on the table, took some food and left."

Frida Kahlo was plagued with health problems throughout her marriage to Rivera. After an operation

Diego Rivera enjoys time with his wife, Frida Kahlo, in the garden of their home.

on her spine in 1946, she was in nearly constant pain. She died in 1954. "July 13, 1954, was the most tragic day of my life," Rivera wrote. "I had lost my beloved Frida forever. . . . Too late now I realized that the most wonderful part of my life had been my love for Frida."

A year after Frida's death, Rivera married Emma Hurtado, the art dealer who handled his paintings. His own health was declining. He had been battling cancer since 1952. In 1957, a stroke paralyzed his right arm. Rivera continued to paint using his left hand. He died of heart failure on November 25, 1957.

Rivera's finest paintings are sweeping **panoramas** with figures larger than life. The legend of Diego Rivera is also larger than life—made so by the wild stories he enjoyed telling, the political passion he couldn't keep quiet, and the controversies he loved to create.

Before he died, the United States was gripped by a fear of Communists. During this period, city officials in Detroit suggested that Rivera's famous mural at the Institute of Arts should be removed. The Detroit Art Commission studied the mural and wrote an open letter to the City Council: "There is no question that Rivera enjoys making trouble," the commissioners stated. "But this man, who often behaves like a child, is one of the outstanding talents of the Western

Diego Rivera and Emma Hurtado shortly after their marriage in 1955.

Diego Rivera at his home in Coyoacán, Mexico, in 1952.

Hemisphere. . . . In the Detroit frescoes we have one of the best as well as one of the most serious of his works. No other artist in the world could have painted murals of such magnitude and force." The paintings remain on the institute's walls for all the world to admire.

1886: Diego Rivera is born in Guanajuato, Mexico, on December 2.

1892: The Rivera family moves from Guanajuato to Mexico City.

1897: Diego Rivera enrolls at the San Carlos Academy of Fine Arts in Mexico City.

1907: Diego Rivera goes to Europe to study art.

1910: Rivera returns briefly to Mexico. Mexican revolutionaries overthrow President Porfirio Díaz.

1911: Diego Rivera and Angelina Beloff are married in Paris.

1914: World War I begins in Europe.

1921: Rivera returns to Mexico after 14 years in Europe.

1922: Diego Rivera and Lupe Marín are married.

1923: Rivera joins the Communist Party in Mexico City.

1929: Diego Rivera and Frida Kahlo are married.

1930: Rivera travels to San Francisco to paint a mural.

1932: Rivera refuses to remove Lenin's portrait from a mural at Rockefeller Center and the Rockefellers have the painting destroyed.

1938: Rivera helps Leon Trotsky obtain political asylum in Mexico. Diego Rivera and Frida Kahlo divorce, then remarry in December.

1942: Rivera begins work on the building that will house his vast collection of pre-Columbian artwork.

1954: Frida Kahlo dies on July 13.

1957: Diego Rivera dies on November 24.

centennial (sen-TEN-ee-uhl) A centennial is a 100-year anniversary. In 1910, Mexico held a centennial celebration.

exploited (eks-PLOY-ted) Someone or something that is exploited is used unfairly for someone else's benefit. In many of Rivera's paintings, the rich exploited the poor.

exuberant (eg-ZOO-bur-uhnt) To be exuberant is to be wildly excited and happy. Rivera described Mexico as an exuberant land.

frenzy (FREN-zee) A frenzy is an intense, desperate hurry. Sometimes Rivera painted in a frenzy.

frescoes (FRESS-kohz) Frescoes are paintings done on wet plaster. Many of the works that Rivera admired were frescoes.

liberated (LIB-uh-ra-ted) To be liberated is to be set free. Rivera believed that Communism would liberate the poor.

literacy (LIT-ur-uh-see) Literacy is the ability to read and write. Jose Vasconcelos promoted literacy in Mexico.

murals (MYU-ruhlz) Murals are large paintings on the walls of a building. Diego Rivera is famous for painting murals.

panoramas (pan-uh-RAM-uhz) Panoramas are wide views of a landscape or scene. Many of Rivera's murals are historical panoramas.

pre-Columbian (pree-koh-LUM-bee-uhn) Pre-Columbian art dates to the time before Columbus sailed to the Americas. Diego Rivera gathered a vast collection of pre-Columbian artwork.

Renaissance (REN-uh-sahnss) The Renaissance was the period in Europe from the 1300s to 1500s in which art, music, and learning flourished. Rivera greatly admired the painters of Renaissance Italy.

textile (TEK-stile) A textile is a woven or knitted cloth. In Veracruz, Mexico, textile workers went on strike for better wages.

Books

Bankston, John. *Diego Rivera*. Bear, Del.: Mitchell Lane, 2003.

Holland, Gini, and Gary Rees (illustrator). *Diego Rivera*. Austin, Tex.: Steck-Vaughn, 1997.

Schaefer, Adam. *Diego Rivera*. Chicago: Heinemann, 2003.

Vazquez, Sarah. *Diego Rivera: An Artist's Life*. Austin, Tex.: Steck-Vaughn, 1998.

Web Sites

Visit our home page for lots of links about Diego Rivera:

http://www.childsworld.com/links.html

Note to Parents, Teachers, and Librarians:
We routinely check our Web links to make sure they're safe, active sites—
so encourage your readers to check them out!

About the Author

Deborah Kent grew up in Little Falls, New Jersey, and received her bachelor's degree from Oberlin College. She earned a master's degree from Smith College School for Social Work and worked as a social worker before becoming a full-time writer. She is the author of 18 young-adult novels and more than 50 nonfiction titles for children. She lives in Chicago with her husband, children's author R. Conrad Stein, and their daughter, Janna.

Index